boil

coin

join

soil

point

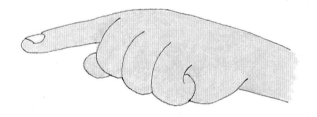

noise

hoist

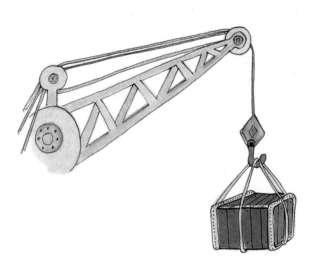

Blending – the Key to Reading

The main skill in reading is blending. Blending is the putting together of letter sounds to make a word. Encourage the child to say the sounds of the letters and to listen for the word. To begin with, you may have to do this together. The ability to blend sounds can take some time for children to master. In developing this skill, a 'little and often' approach usually works best.

Hints on Blending:

- It can help children to hear the word if they say the first sound slightly louder than the others, e.g. ***p***-*i*-*g*.

- In order to hear the word, children must say the letter sounds fairly quickly.

Light Type

As a guide for new readers, light type is used for letters that should not be sounded out, such as the ‹e› in 'house'. Light type occurs in only a few books.